To Nick
Thanks
support,

Lovelorn and Rudderless

[MEANDERINGS #1]

David Green

2016

simplepigeon

- short works of oblique travelography -

ISBN: 0955070023
ISBN-13: 978-0955070020

"The use of travelling is to regulate imagination by reality, and instead of thinking how things may be, to see them as they are."

Samuel Johnson

"It's not the *real* world."

My Mother.

CONTENTS

PROLOGUE

It was the year 2000. Computers everywhere had not crashed. The world had not ended. For reasons obscured by hindsight, I was living in London. A two tube commute to my dull and uninspiring job took an hour each way. City life was wearing me down and fault lines were appearing in my friendship group, the inevitable outcome of too much bed-hopping. I was done with the norms. What to do? Escape London. Escape England. Escape Europe. I bought a round the world ticket.

Like a first love affair, bringing this first grand adventure to an end after a mere twelve months seemed nothing short of cataclysmic. So I threw the ticket away and dragged it out to fifteen months. And then dragged it further, to eighteen months, just long enough to find myself broke twice over and exhausted, shivering behind a hostel sofa and trying not to sneeze lest I be caught trespassing.

What follows is an account of the rudderless trajectory of a lovelorn idiot trying his best to not go home.

1 LOVE AT FIRST SIGHT

She turned around. Our eyes met. BOOM.

Electricity. Inner wibbles.

But before all that, Sydney, miserable, in the middle of winter.

After nine months of solo adventuring throughout South East Asia, Australia's first city seemed drab and lifeless by comparison. The suburb where I was hostelling reminded me a little of home, which could have been comforting, except it was colder, wetter and greyer than the North West and I didn't know anybody. The closest friend I had was my jumper, a bobbly affair I'd managed to keep hold of, unlike all of my t-shirts and a carousel of hats that had been lost along the way. The air was leaking out of my adventure balloons; I decided to move on quickly, high-tailing it to Melbourne on my last reserves of energy. A friend there had promised to put me up and get me on my feet. I'll call him Jim.

I met Jim on the first day of my travels at the immigration queue back in Bangkok after a very nervy flight. At thirty three thousand feet with Turkey blinking beneath me it suddenly dawned on me that I had no plan. I would see Angkor in Cambodia. I would slowboat the Mekong in Laos. I would take a canoe out on Danau Toba in Sumatra. That was it. Aside from those three intentions, I had nothing. I didn't even know where I'd be sleeping on the first night. Luckily the airline had bumped me to business class so the sudden rush of blood and cortisol that accompanied the reality panic coincided with complimentary cashew nuts and champagne.

The bloke sitting next to me was a real businessman who'd spent half his life in Thailand. He assuaged my fears by telling me that Thailand was 'a doddle'. I know that now, but back then I had no idea what to expect. I'd never tasted non-temperate air or been exposed to temperatures or humidities above an average balmy English summer or the south of France. In all my travels and adventures since, nothing has come close to the intensity of that first moment when the glass doors slid apart and the stinky, wet, exotic heat of a tropical Bangkok morning smothered me.

Jim was standing in front of me in the customs line. We went through together and jumped in the same taxi. He was with a woman whose name I forget. They were friends, not lovers. He'd been in England for seven years and was breaking up his journey home with a stint of travel. The three of us got drunk on the Khao San Road at seven in the morning, flabbergasted by the alien heat and the sheer madness of all the human traffic. Wasters. Wizards. Queens. Hippies. Goddesses. Drifters. Dreamers. Dropouts. Of course we stayed too long. And drank too much. Later that day we found a room: myself, Jim, and the girl he was travelling with. It had one bed – three of us in one big bed, all drunk and jet-lagged and confused. We bobbed on the surface of sleep for a few hours and drifted back to consciousness with steaming tropical hangovers. I woke first to find my head inches away from the girl's bottom. She farted as I regained consciousness. The experience was exactly as horrible as it sounds, all warm and fetid and spicy. Despite these inauspicious beginnings, I stuck with Jim and his farty-bottom friend for a few weeks and we trekked together in Chiang Mai, riding elephants, bamboo rafting, doing our national dances in Karen villages and participating in all the usual funfair nonsense that 'authentic' tourist treks involve.

Afterwards we went our separate ways and he gave me his email with a promise that I would always be welcome at his family home in Melbourne if I ever needed a place to recuperate or re-inflate. I called him from Sydney. Then I called the airline and changed my tickets. I swam to Jim like a castaway to a raft in my airless seas.

My original plan for Australia was to become a cowboy. Yee-haw! I'd never ridden a horse. I had no experience with cows. I'd never thrown a lasso, or worn a gallon hat, or tramped around in big boots with spurs. I wasn't particularly gnarly or rugged and I certainly couldn't chew tobacco, bolt down half bottles of moonshine or shoot a can off a wall from any number of paces. But I had read a book by Cormac McCarthy and that was enough to convince me that all of these skills would come naturally, that they were latent within me as if I was born with an inner cowboy waiting to be expressed. Somewhere in that enormous country too, there was a horse waiting for me to saddle her up and canter through endless sunsets. Throughout it's thus far uneventful life, a nagging feeling would have arisen from time to time, a sense that something was missing, that somebody was coming to fill that absence in her sense of purpose and allow her to step into her true nature, as she would do for me. The indescribable bond of friendship between a man and his steed. I was saved from the inevitable disappointment of being rubbish at all of these things when, to my complete surprise, my plans were derailed by falling in love at first sight with Jim's sister.

It began like this: Jim introduced me to his mother.

'Hello, nice to meet you.'

And his father.

'Hello, nice to meet you too.'

And then to his sister, who I shall call Cerys.

She turned around. Our eyes met. BOOM. Electricity. Inner wibbles. Love at first sight. At the dinner table that night the air between us seemed to bend and bow and fizzle with a weird blue light. This sounds melodramatic, perhaps even ridiculous, but the rest of the family noticed it too. Jim's mother tried to normalise the atmosphere with talk of physics, but there was no silencing this crackling static in the air between us. When everybody eventually went to bed, Cerys and I were left alone on the sofa talking, watching videos (that she had made), and sheepishly giving each other head scratches. She disappeared at around 1am and returned in her nightdress, a black lace number that blended with her hair and gave her pale complexion more expression. Before the night ended, we had already kissed.

She was 18 and I was 23. She had a boyfriend. I met him one night when we went clubbing for Jim's birthday. It being a special occasion and me being new to the area, I bought some Day-Glo orange pants from a charity shop to make a good impression on the ravers and didn't say 'no' when Jim offered pick-me-ups for the party, only they weren't pick-me-ups at all. They were more like slap-you-downs and everybody felt rubbish. Half way through the night I found Cerys slumped by the wall outside worried that the pick-me-up slap-you-downs were making hay with the medication she was taking for panic attacks. I'd had one once. Like everybody else, when my heart started racing and my chest went numb and the sweats came, I assumed it was a case of spontaneous sudden death taking hold. Of course it wasn't, and I recovered fully. That was on the underground, in London. Not knowing what was happening to me, but being aware of my sudden awkwardness, my discomfort and all the sweating, my fellow passengers seemed put out by my odd behaviour, as if the drama I was making was in some way offensive to them. Maybe they had panic attacks all the time. Maybe it was normal on the London tube and making a fuss was considered poor form. I learned to notice and control the symptoms after that incident and, thankfully, never had another one. Cerys was unable to do so. She wrestled with the feelings, getting all tangled up and caught, making the attacks worse and more frequent. We were still sharing our experiences when her boyfriend came out of the club and found us. I explained that Cerys wasn't feeling well and left them to it. The night went on. Nobody had a particularly good time – how can you when you've no idea what's going on inside you, which biological process are being interfered with, what damage might be being done by the unidentified particles you've thrown into the mix. There are many different directions to travel in, some more rewarding than others. On the way home I lost feeling in my arm. One minute it was there, the next it was gone. I had to shake it out. I wasn't even lying on it or sitting on it. Jim lost consciousness in the taxi and was convinced afterwards that he hadn't simply fallen asleep - he'd passed out. Our mind-body connections were screwy but we all made it home. The bizarre birthday party finally came to an end and with it my short-lived phase of wearing Day-Glo orange pants.

A few weeks later Cerys was single. Then she was going out with me. One night when I was tootling ineptly on the piano, Jim's mother came in and sat down next to me on the piano stool. She told me with a conspiratorial tone that 'in this house the universe is unbounded'. A seemingly innocuous reference to our earlier conversations about physics, this was in fact her way of telling me it would be fine for me to go out with her daughter and move in to her room! A month later Jim was off again, following his travelling nose to Scotland, leaving me at home in his house, living with his family and sleeping with his younger sister. Who knew *that* was waiting around his corner?

Having reluctantly come to the realisation that I was not destined to ride horses or eat beans around campfires, I decided to buy a car and explore the country with my lover alongside me. I had just enough money to buy a half-decent car, but not enough to then fill it with petrol. Or feed myself. Or do anything other than sit in the car and let the world do the driving around me, which in the suburbs of Melbourne would have been terribly underwhelming. I suggested to my father that a short-term loan would carry very little risk for him. I'd buy a car, live the dream with Cerys for six months, then sell the car and give all the proceeds of the sale back to him. Any shortfall could be made up when I returned to what my mother so refreshingly referred to as 'the real world'. Despite his normally cautious and canny temper, he agreed to my terms and transferred the cash.

I opted for a panel van (also called a 'shaggin' wagon', I later found out), and trawled the papers for a suitable example. After inspecting a few with my unprofessional eyes, I ended up handing over a five hundred dollar deposit to a short bloke with beady eyes and a balding pate who claimed to be the organiser of the biggest swing parties in Australia, not to mention managing a very talented, tough and soon-to-be-successful Libyan kick boxer. We shook hands. I gave him the cash. Off I went. On closer inspection by folk more qualified than me, I was told a few days later that the car had a reasonably healthy engine, the gearbox was in good working order, and the tyres were in decent nick. All encouraging news. The chassis however had been stitched together from more than one car and the extensive rust in some key areas was severe enough to warrant extreme caution by all but the most foolhardy of idiots. It might, I was told, be the end of me.

I'd already parted with the deposit cash. And I'd shaken a hand. I'd never bought a car before and I didn't really know what I was doing, what to look for, what questions to ask. I should have judged his character better, but I was green back then and too readily taken in by people who had acquired more street smarts than I had. I asked for my money back, rather sheepishly, keenly aware of the Libyan kick boxer looming over the dodgy fellow from a life-size poster on the wall behind him. His gloves were up, his head down, his lips bulging from the mouth-guard, muscles ripped and rippling. The dark angry eyes of this thug were boring into me, telling me in a brutish way that my appeals were hopeless and I should probably take a battering for the trouble I'd caused. The deposit was not refundable, my beady-eyed friend told me. I tried to insist, to implore, to ingratiate, to impose my will, but he was too canny for me at every turn and every strategy failed. In the end he was pissed off and I somehow felt guilty about it, even though he was the one selling the lame duck and I was the one he nearly screwed. I gathered up the frayed ends of my tail, stuck it firmly between my legs and scarpered, but I wasn't finished with him yet. Later that day I rang citizen's advice and told them I'd been taken advantage of.

"What an outrage," I said. "Me, a guest in this lovely country… treated this way."

The guy on the other end of the phone laughed at me, told me I shouldn't be doing business if I couldn't do business. He didn't care that old beady eyes was selling death traps to unsuspecting idiots, so that was the end of that. No epic journey across the continent for Cerys and I. Five hundred bucks blown.

I should have returned what was left of the money to my father straight away but he told me to keep hold it for a while to help me get on my feet. Cerys and I ended up taking a flat in the city and tried living like real people for a while. She found work in a café, left in the afternoon and came home late most nights smelling of pizza. We spent the mornings in bed. I spent the afternoons trawling second hand bookshops doing research for my first novel, scouring the shelves for any titles that dealt with music and its relationship to mathematics, psychology, metaphysics, history… anything beyond music's own subject. I was writing short stories and making modest inroads into publication, applying for writing retreats, doing a few gigs each week and playing guitar for a lovely feminist lesbian singer-songwriter whose bathroom was covered floor to ceiling with nude Madonna posters. I was living off what little funds I had left and the money my Dad had lent me to buy the car, and that money was running out.

It sounds grand. In truth I was being a bum. But I was in love and I was writing a book, so being a bum somehow seemed justified. I tell my father now that without that money, my first novel would never have been written, which is to some extent true. When he thinks about that money, he doesn't see my first novel. He sees five hundred bucks lost to another pocket and a shiny guitar that in his opinion should probably have stayed in the showroom where it belonged instead of coming into my possession. But as Khalil Gibran writes: 'When love beckons to you, follow him.' It turns out there hadn't been a horse waiting for me all this time in Australia, but a guitar.

I found it the day after I became a crime-fighting superhero in Tasmania.

2 CRIME FIGHTING SUPERHERO

Who would crash a plane into Queenstown?

The round-the-world ticket was about to expire so I decided to squeeze in a two-week trip to Tasmania and then throw it away. Before leaving England I'd pre-booked some voluntary work with the Australian Trust for Conservation Volunteers and found I was able to transfer this to Tasmania too, so I'd get free accommodation whilst I was there. Cerys stayed in Melbourne and I headed off for a mini-adventure with no great expectations. To my surprise Hobart reminded me even more of home, but not the Nottingham of my University days –Hobart was more of a northern town, a Wigan, or a Preston. Here I was on the other side of the world and everything was eerily similar. Of course there was the Southern Ocean, a turbulent, wolfish sea compared with the waters that lap against the shores of Northern England.

The volunteer group was mostly European, made up of people who, like me, had booked round-the-world-tickets and had allowed the travel agent to convince them that having something planned, anything really, would make life easier in the antipodes. The leader of the group was a 23-

year-old who owned some forest on the south coast, had a built a house using his own trees and drove a vehicle that reminded me simultaneously of a relic from an ancient war and a futuristic space buggy. The wheels were as tall as I was high and it used its own weight in fuel on a daily basis, but it was exciting to drive in. We planted some trees and destroyed swathes of pernicious aloe vera that hugged the effluent waste lakes from an industrial complex, something to do with mines, or the processing of whatever was being dug from them. Delightful work. Aloe vera is a prized and very expensive botanical in England but in Australia it is treated like a mere weed. It's funny how one culture's flower is another's weed. It's funny that there are any weeds at all, and that we look down on them as bad creatures, given that a weed is nothing more than a very successful plant. I suppose they're bullies. And they screw things up for farmers.

We were staying in static caravans near Queenstown, an uninspiring town in the middle of the country that seemed to be mostly about the mines. A few other groups were staying on the same site, but they were mostly local, Tasmanian and some mainlanders. One morning I stumbled into the boss's caravan for some coffee and sensed something unusual in the mood, an intensely attentive atmosphere that in my blurry condition I couldn't immediately pin down. Everybody was looking at the television, so I looked too, just in time to see the first World Trade Centre tower crumble and collapse. Like everybody else in the world, my first reaction was one of sheer disbelief. I've been told that deja-vu is a bit like a short circuit in the brain, whereby the wires for memory and sensory input get crossed and one becomes confused with the other, so current experience feels like a memory. The towers coming down gave rise to a similar feeling, except in this case all the wires from memory led directly to scenes out of ridiculous action movies. This was a definite feeling of unreality. Though everybody was shocked, they all continued with their morning routines, making coffee and readying themselves for another day of voluntary labour. When they eventually left for the effluent lakes I insisted on staying behind to watch the drama unfold and figure out what had happened and what it meant.

By the time the first group returned in the afternoon I was still shell-shocked by the events and mollified by the tedious 24-hour news coverage, despite rolling in caffeine. On a more positive note, I was grateful for where I was - the furthest place from anywhere. Who would crash a plane into Queenstown?

This first group back were all Australians. They occupied caravans on the other side of the park, but we'd had no contact with them. One of them sauntered over and smilingly asked me if I wanted to join them for a BBQ and I jumped at the opportunity. This turned out to be my first brush with what became a disappointingly recurring theme of my travels 'down under': racism. Cultures are funny creatures. I dislike generalisations about people or places, and when I hear one expressed, I react angrily, drawing more conclusions about the speaker than I do of the culture they are casting a wide net of collective judgement upon. But there's no getting around it. In Australia, the ugly head of racism kept rearing its head in ways that were unsettling and offensive. Maybe some people there are simply more honest about feelings that lie simmering beneath the surface of all cultures. An Indian friend of mine once told me that everyone – meaning every culture, but to some extent every person – is racist, that it's natural and inherent with a genuine psychological basis. Plenty of aspects of character are natural, but it doesn't mean we should invite them all in.

On this occasion, as New York was filling with dust and the world was contemplating panic, I found myself chugging beers and waiting for the meat to brown while one lad regaled us all with a scatty monologue that veered with virtuosity from one random subject to the next. He was cracking us all up. I forget what he was actually talking about, but I do remember the momentum of my laughter carrying me into a distinctly awkward place, and what he said there is not easily forgotten. He shared his master plan with the assembled crowd; he was going to sleep with every single woman in Tasmania. Not an unusual ambition for a healthy young male in touch with his natural urges, but his reasoning was exceptional. When asked why, his eyes narrowed and he raised his hands in the air like an orator delivering the killer line:

"To purify this land. To breed out the last of the wogs, the niggers and the japs."

Ha ha ha… eh? You must be joking? His eyes were beaming. He kept his hand aloft. I cast my gaze quickly over the crowd.

"You must be joking," one of the girls said, and I breathed a premature sigh of relief, but she followed it up with: "You're an eighth wog yerself. How can you clean this place up?"

Did I let out another laugh? If I did it was nervous, but everyone else was laughing, so maybe I didn't. The settling of Tasmania had been a genocidal enterprise, I reminded myself, but that was all a long time ago and societies move on. A key aspect of the Australian Prime Minister's election campaign at that time drew heavily on public sentiment towards refugees that were arriving against all odds from terrible places and finding themselves on the shores of Australia, hoping for asylum and respite from persecution. The popular choice, and the policy on which the incumbent Prime Minister was elected, was to either send them on to barren islands in the Pacific or hold them in rudimentary camps in the interior. In a sensational and perverse statement of injustice, several of the women held in these camps famously stitched their children's mouths shut in protest at their lack of voice and the lack of humanity being shown to them.

When I was fruit picking deep in the interior, three Liberians kept 'losing' their picking bag and had to pay new deposits for replacements. They confided in me that the bags disappeared from their rooms. They were taken, probably by the paymasters. One day the lunches arrived and we were one short. The last picker in was one of the Liberians. When he asked for his lunch the 'gangers' told him there was none and laughed him away. He protested, but was laughed at again. As he turned, shoulders slumped and brow furrowed, one of the gangers chortled to the others that 'niggers never do any work anyway, they're useless.' If no work was being done, then why was he the last one in for lunch and why was he sweating so profusely when he arrived? On that occasion, I acted, making clear my feelings about allowing somebody – anybody – to perform such demanding work in such demanding heat without eating. Another lunch was eventually brought. The gangers regarded me with a sort of half-interested contempt, but the sight of the defeated Liberian walking away from the gangers stuck with me and still makes me angry. These attitudes were rife on the farms. Toilet cubicles were courts on which racist graffiti tennis matches were played out. On one wall you'd see a slur on the blacks, with a counter-slur on the opposing wall. New slurs would appear over time, and cubicles that hadn't been cleaned for a while had turned into lists, repositories of colour-based abuse.

One wonders to what extent a national psyche, formed through habits and historical precedents beyond the control or influence of an individual, can infiltrate the psyche of the individual and create there a substrate on which their own behaviours must accrete. In the endless back and forth of the 'nature vs. nurture' debate someone famously once said that we are definitely one hundred per cent nature and definitely one hundred per cent nurture. Being British I often notice the shadow of Empire in the attitudes of my kin and even in some aspects of my own unquestioned attitudes. Nobody is proud of the legacy and the manifestations of it are almost always unpalatable, but like habits that form in early life, they can't always be easily removed.

When you travel you come across national stereotypes all the time and there's nothing more disappointing than when somebody shows their national self in colours so bright that you find it difficult to see through to the individual. I make an effort to meet everyone as anyone, and my first encounters with concrete generalisations in travelling communities were deeply unsettling, but over time, and in spite of my ideals, a process of statistical averaging tended to solidify these apocryphal and seemingly prejudicial characteristics into real traits, sorted by nationality. The thought of giving examples here in writing makes me feel uneasy, as if by committing my experiences to paper I will be judged as somebody who subscribes to this crass way of categorising people. Perhaps there is a cohort of people across the world, in every nation, that collectively creates and sustains these national traits by adhering to them without reflection or awareness. The numbers wouldn't need to be large. The human mind needs only to experience a few examples of something it expects to come across in order to make a rule that doesn't necessarily bear any relation to reality, designed as it is to find patterns from the limited amount of information it can process. Did I do this in Australia? Did I join a few dots into an impression that bore no relation to the broader picture, like an astrologer blithely declaring that a few scattered stars light-years apart and in no way specifically related are in fact Pegasus or The Great Bear? Racism exists everywhere, and some psychologists insist that we are predisposed to bias on the basis of familiarity, but if it is inherent in us all, for some there is a cultural imperative to resist, to overwhelm or to overcome such baseless notions. For others there is a lazy indulgence.

Cerys' mother told me that 95% of people who go on trips into the aboriginal territories are conscientious white Australians reacting to deep-seated feelings that are linked to the 'sins of their fathers': the continental land grab; the subsequent hunting of the indigenous people; the on-going undercurrent of discrimination. She made a joke that no Australian was a descendant of a rapist or a murderer, that all the criminal great grandfathers had been caught stealing bread to feed starving families in Liverpool, and had been thrown onto the prison ships unjustly, victims of social inequality, martyrs if you will, crushed beneath the wheel of aristocracy and Empire. Whether their forebears stole bread or sodomised the King, the modern Australian isn't any more culpable for these crimes than I am for the Opium Wars or the industrial slave trade, or indeed for the injustice of the forced deportations that led to the first wave of modern Australians. In much the same way that original sin curses every Catholic, History blesses every one of us with different flavours of guilt at birth. All we can do is live our lives by our own values in full understanding that we did not place the yoke on our own necks, believing that through our behaviours and actions we will gradually slip the yoke and walk free from its burdens. If, like the young man at the BBQ, we perpetuate the same attitudes that inspired the atrocities of the past, we become worse than our forefathers, because no matter how tenuous their convictions may appear with the benefit of hindsight, we can never lay claim to the same excuses they had.

I left Queenstown at the end of the week and headed for Launceston, the second biggest town in Tasmania behind Hobart, its capital. I checked in to a hostel hoping to do nothing but loaf around, chill, read and relax. I was reading Brave New World and 1984 back to back, which was a surreal experience that led to me looking over my shoulder more than usual and wondering frequently if everything was as it appeared to be. I read the last line of

1984 on the roof terrace of the hostel and at the precise moment I put the book down and gazed out over the skyline to take in the denouement, a ventilation pipe, kinked at ninety degrees with a fin mounted on it to turn it away from the wind, swung in a breeze to point directly at me and rested in that position. It was impeccably timed to send a shiver up my spine.

Aside from the attentions of Big Brother and the occasional bouts of paranoia that this inevitably stirred, everything went to plan with my relaxing until fate decreed that I would find myself thrust into the action of a live crime spree, and that I would be cast, rather unwittingly I might add, in the role of the crime fighting super hero.

There were three bunk beds in my room. I was on the bottom of one. Another guy was on the bottom of another. The rest were empty. I awoke with an awareness of danger, a certainty that something was wrong in the world, but I had no idea what and I was wary of it being another case of Orwell getting inside my psyche and making me think weirdly. Turning in my bed I beheld a dark shape, looming, the shape of a man, a large man, in a long coat, one hand outstretched holding what looked like a pair of trousers. It didn't move, this man-shaped shadow. I didn't move either, for a moment. My eyes adjusted and I realised it really was a pair of trousers hanging from the hand of a shape that truly was a real, live, looming man.

'Those are my trousers." I said, not entirely awake. It seemed apposite to the circumstances to state this fact.

'You've got my jacket.' The man said. Had this been true, his statement would have matched mine perfectly in tone, appropriateness and candour. But I didn't have his jacket. I looked at the trousers again. They were definitely trousers. My trousers. And I didn't have anybody's jacket. Were we taking part in the same conversation?

"You've got my jacket," he said again. It made no sense. I reached forwards and took the trousers. He let go of them without a struggle. I looked at them closely. My trousers. And put them on my bed. Now I was leaning on my arm looking up at the looming man in the long-coat.

"I'm just trying to find somewhere to sleep," the guy said, but this was the same guy who'd just told me twice that I had his jacket, so could I trust him?

His voice was even, neither aggressive nor meek, just matter of fact. I said something about him leaving the room and continuing his quest for sleep somewhere else, and I would just turn over and go back to my own sleep and that would be that. One strange conversation, one accidental but temporary shift in ownership of a pair of trousers (that wouldn't fit him), and nothing more to say. He mumbled something about his imaginary jacket and, to my relief, left the room. I turned over, put my head on the pillow and for a moment I almost convinced myself that I could just go back to sleep and that would be that, but before I knew it I was on my feet, turning the door handle and unthinkingly walking out of the room. Into what? A corner. Around which I had no idea what I would find. I wasn't yet awake.

The front door was to my right, twenty paces away. To go up the stairs you had to double back on yourself at the front door. The reception counter was next to the stairs, and a small office was housed under the stairs at the end of a narrow corridor that led away behind the counter. Sticking out of this office I saw somebody's arse. It was a builder's arse, the cleavage bulging out of low-hung jeans. I took this in without thought and walked upstairs. The kitchen was floor to ceiling glass-fronted fridges on two walls, with open-plan counters on the other two. The looming shape from my room was peering into the glass fridges. I walked to the sink, turned on the tap and filled a glass with water. He was behind me now, diagonally across from me, in the corner, thankfully not close enough to stop me reaching the stairs again. When the water hit my lips and I felt it's cold wetness, all the pieces of this strange evening fell together and made sense. Two rather large and rough looking men were breaking into the hostel. Nobody else knew this. I'd somehow positioned myself in my semi-somnambulant way at the far end of the hostel, at the furthest point from the door, and these two men, criminals to an unknown extent, one of which was almost certainly challenged in the faculty of reason, now stood between me and everything safe - my room, other people, and the exit. Luckily I was still sleepy enough to not fully appreciate the potential danger I was in. With no plan I turned and started walking with my glass of water. The man at the fridge was looking at me with a confused expression of intimidating befuddlement.

"Good luck finding your bed," I said, or something equally inane but tied to his fantasy.

As I turned to the stairs a rush of electricity shot up my back, like I used to get when my parents made me get coal from the coal shed and I had to turn the light off and walk through the garage in the dark. The other man was at the bottom of the stairs, standing stock still, regarding me with violence. I somehow denied this fact to myself, smiled in a sleepy way as I walked down the stairs and gave him a simple, 'Evening mate.'

I walked around him, turned the corner and headed for the dormitories, the final stretch of unsafe ground before I could get into my room and lock it. The rush went up my back again but I kept walking. As I turned the door handle I shot another glance back the way I'd come. The man had moved a few feet to his right to afford a better view of me walking to the door and had resumed his stock-still standing and his violent eyes. I whooshed through, locked the door behind me and listened intently. No footsteps.

Safe in my room it dawned on me how foolishly unthinking I'd been in my half asleep. I was now fully awake. I pulled a bunk bed to the door and blocked it. Then I woke the other guy and explained what was happening. He had a phone but it wasn't working. I climbed into the top bunk and lit a cigarette under the fire alarm. Nothing happened. I took the bin up and made a little fire out of another cigarette but still nothing happened. Eventually we decided to go back out again and cross the hall to the manager's room. It was no more than a few meters. Either the two men would be waiting outside for us or my weird confrontation would have startled them, and they'd be long gone. We both hoped for the latter and resolved to take action.

Turning the lock as quietly as possible, we eased the door towards us and peered out. The corridor was empty. We didn't move. My ears strained against the silence but found nothing, so I crept out, crossed the hall and tapped on the manager's door. He came out almost immediately and I hurriedly explained the situation. He shook off his sleep and called the police as we marched through the empty building looking for long-gone crooks.

When the police arrived I was proclaimed a hero. The thieves had already rifled through two other hostels undetected, but their spree had now come to an end because of my trousers. The suspects were apprehended on their way through a nearby park. As they ran for their freedom they emptied their pockets and cast all their contraband into the bushes. I was asked to itemise my losses, but I hadn't checked, so I ducked back into my room to do an inventory. They'd taken my vanilla shampoo. And some underpants. There's no way my underpants would have fitted either of them. For that matter, my trousers would have been equally ill fitting. Strange burglars.

The next morning I was greeted by a coffee-wielding manager who informed me that I would not have to pay a penny for the rest of my stay at the hostel, that he and the other hostel managers were grateful for my brave efforts in bringing to an end the spree that had blighted the fair town of Launceston. I half-expected the keys to the city, but alas they were not forthcoming. I reminded him that what might have seemed like bravery to him was in fact mere half-asleepness and a complete absence of any capacity for strategic thinking, but he laughed this off and went on with his business.

3 A REALLY IRISH ACCENT

Yoer fuckin' stooopid.

I went walking around the streets of this now-safe city and stumbled upon a guitar shop. I ambled in thinking it might be nice to spend some time playing on a decent guitar instead of the piece of junk I'd been carrying around with me since Thailand. To my complete surprise, it happened again. I fell in love at first sight.

The guitar in question was a Takamine EF-407. This means nothing to a non-guitarist. How can I describe it? It had a rosewood fretboard with mother of pearl inlays. The body was a solid top (single piece) of Japanese maple. The headstock made it look like a Spanish guitar because the machine heads were pointed away and behind the body, and the body was smaller than most acoustics, further compounding the impression of classical Spanishness. But it was steel-strung. It sounded deep and thick and warm and lovely. When you struck the harmonics and held the body close to your ear, the fade of resonance went on forever, like a baby grand piano. It was semi-acoustic and when you plugged it in it became even warmer.

On the graphic equaliser it had a dial labelled simply

'Exciter.' It looked and sounded divine. On the one hand I felt helpless, drawn by some pseudo-cosmic thread into partnership with this instrument, and on the other hand, well, I was a crime-fighting superhero. Superheroes need sidekicks. And they deserve some reward for the sacrifices they make. The money from the failed car purchase would see me through a few months of rent. Aside from that, I had £600 of emergency fly-home funds. This was surprisingly close to the sum required to make the sidekick mine. But I was about to throw my ticket away, making the potential of an emergency very present and real. Sometimes you've just got to ignore sense and do what feels right. I called a friend in England and asked him to price-check it for me, but I'd already made my mind up. I bought the guitar. Then I called my mum.

"Hi Mum… sitting down??? Excellent. Yes, all is well. Hey, great news: I've bought another guitar."

My mother grew up in Ireland but has lived in England for most of her life. Her real Irish accent normally lies dormant under a mere Celtic twang, but when she gets excited or angry, the twang gives way to the voice she was born with. She was well used to my spontaneous guitar-buying habits. I'd left five guitars in her loft. But none of those guitars had essentially trapped me in another continent. Of the two triggers I had the feeling it wasn't excitement that took her back to her roots on this occasion.

"Ah Deeavid, yoer fuckin' stoopid," she said.

Fair enough. I should mention that the guitar is still with me thirteen years later, that she changed the way I play in ways I couldn't have imagined beforehand and that our partnership in music has always been fruitful, creative and devoid of any heartbreak or difficulty. The same cannot be said for Cerys and our relationship.

When the plane thudded back down in Melbourne I took my round-the-world ticket and with great ceremony dumped it into a bin as I strode out into the world with my love-at-first-sight-sidekick under my arm, heading for the flat where my love-at-first-sight-girlfriend was waiting for me. Aside from being truly broke, everything seemed rosy in my life and my heels clicked along the pavement as the sun smiled high above me in a blessed blue sky. A month or so later, and for reasons not entirely clear to either of us, the magic between Cerys and I fizzled out. Essentially, we were living in different worlds. She was about to go to University in Australia. I was about to go home, albeit in a protracted stagger and without much enthusiasm. Her panic attacks hadn't improved. If anything, they'd gotten worse and more frequent, and I didn't know how to help her. One night she came to a gig I was playing but we had to leave before I played because she got hit by one. I didn't understand. I was twenty-three. Most men are idiots at twenty-three, full of rattling ego and self-interest and very little wisdom or empathy. I sometimes look back at that love-at-first-sight relationship and feel a twinge of regret, or shame, because maybe I didn't treat her as well as I tell myself I did. Maybe I just needed her around to pump the air back into my adventure balloons. Maybe she needed me for something similar.

A year and a half later I answered the phone in Bristol and heard her voice again. She'd been saving up for a ticket to come to England. She told me it could be used the other way round, that the name could be changed too. I could go back. For a visit, nothing more. Of course I said no. Another year went by and I found out that she'd been in hospital for a serious operation, that the panic attacks had been linked to a developing tumour in her brain. Another year or two went by and she married. She had a child and moved into the woods with her family. This all made me very happy. One day I opened my email to find a message from her. It began:

Dear Dave, I've been putting back together the pieces of my mind that got scrambled by the tumour and I just wanted you to know that you treated me like shit when we were together...

It didn't go on much further.

Memories are slippery things. Every time we summon one to mind we change it in the process. I've no idea what she remembers and what has been forgotten or taken by the surgeon's knife. I've no idea what our relationship has become to her now, but to me it will always be that first moment, when the air was fizzling with blue light and the space between us seemed to bow and wobble before us. Or sitting outside the club dealing with stuff. Or drinking too much coffee and getting all juddery and giggly at the same time. Staying up late, listening to music, making love. But we were two different people in two different worlds, heading in two different directions, and no matter how intense and incredible our coming together may have been, it was, like most romantic affairs that don't lead to woodland homes and weddings, an affair that outlasted the magic it was inspired by.

She went back to her parent's house. I stayed in the city and looked for a rudder to steer by.

4 NORTH IS NORTH

Guts and determination...

It was around this time that Rob and Jane arrived, an English couple I'd met in Sumatra at the tail end of the Asian leg of the journey. Rob was in fact Welsh, but for the first two weeks of our travels in Sumatra together he somehow managed to maintain an authentic and consistent Yorkshire accent throughout. This was supposedly for my benefit. One evening, sipping beers on the porch as the sun was slipping colourfully into the crater lake of Danau Toba, he turned with a sly grin and told me that in his opinion I hadn't shown him much gratitude for the efforts he had made in alleviating my homesickness. Eh? Then he spoke. Normally. Turns out he'd been affecting a regional accent all along and his real accent was... Welsh. He was from Cardiff, not Leeds, where he'd gone to University, and where I'd assumed he was from. It was impressive that he'd managed to stay so convincingly Northern for so long, and in the company of strangers too, but I think he enjoyed playing with the patois in much the same way I enjoy twanging into Irish every now and then. What could I say? Thanks? I told him I was from Merseyside, which isn't Yorkshire. There's even a Lancashire between Merseyside and Yorkshire, so he was two counties out.

'Aye laddie, but North is North.'

Jane was more straightforward, a sweet girl, earnest, wide-eyed, innocent, full of wonder. When Rob had to take a trip to Singapore to meet a friend, he left me 'in charge' of Jane. He sat me down on the day of his departure and told me that although he didn't know me all that well, he trusted me and was hoping that this trust was well-placed, that I would look after Jane in his absence and not do anything 'funny' while he was away. It was a very serious conversation. I laughed and told him all would be well. There would be no besmirching of his damsel while I was there to defend her honour. So Jane and I spent a night together on the shore of Danau Maninjau. Some crater lakes are so big you don't know you're in them, like Danau Toba, which simply feels like a huge lake. By contrast, Maninjau is small enough for you to feel enclosed in the rim. Although it isn't particularly elevated, the ridgeline and the pronounced cleft at one end of it gives you the impression that the whole thing is raised up in the air like a chalice offered to the gods. It's a very romantic place. Of course I kept my word and refrained from besmirching, but a part of me flew with fantasy that night. We were sitting in easy chairs on the end of the pier watching the night fall, fisherman pulling at their nets, birds swooping around us after their insect prey, reggae music rolling out of the jungle, deepening twilight colours making shapes on a canvas of clouds, drinks in our hands, gentle banter passing back and forth between us. She was a genuine ingénue, unintentionally intriguing and beguiling. Such charms as these normally reside in folk tales and traditionally drive men to bizarre acts of faith or madness. I held it together.

Months later, after a few too many beers, I cornered Rob beneath a street light and demanded to know what brand of devious magic he'd employed to win the heart of his lovely Jane. His eyes narrowed. He held my gaze, looked me right in the soul and spoke with a voice that began in his belly and deepened as it made the journey through his body to his mouth:

'Guts and determination.'

Several months after the adventures of Danau Toba and Maninjau, Rob and Jane flew to Australia and made a beeline for Melbourne to move into my under-occupied and love-forgotten flat. We all had to make money but it was a struggle to find decent work. None of us were particularly qualified in anything. I had a science degree and I'd worked in a housing association in London for a year, but I had no useful experience of the world whatsoever. Graduates without experience are like pointless grassy hummocks in the landscape of work. University has taught us how to make cheese toasties, stay up late, be cool in one way or another (or at least think we are), cram stuff into short-term memory and blag our way through tutorials, none of which is of much use in employment. Perhaps this is not true of all graduates. It is true of most of the ones I know. It was true for the three of us.

Rob had the most success, perhaps due to his linguistic flexibility and the bonhomie that this can engender in those he hoodwinks. He wrangled a company car from a door-to-door sales company that we almost made money through, but it turned out to be a dodgy pyramid scheme and led nowhere. He persevered longer than I did, partly due to the fact that they'd given him a car and he was enjoying ragging it around the city, but I gave up quickly and stayed at home for a while making inventively designed monopoly and chess sets out of odds and ends with Jane. We cut things up and stuck them together and made things up and took great pride in our achievements, though the world was largely indifferent to our enterprises and we soon lost interest. Somewhere around this time Jane and Rob had a bust up and I came home to find Rob punching the light bulb out of it's socket on our porch.

'Why are you punching our light bulb?' I asked him. But he'd already gone. Inside Jane was packing a case to go who knows where. It all died down and was forgotten, but we took it as a symptom of our malaise. We needed to get productive, focused, 'on it'; we were dawdling through life.

I found another job selling advertising space in a calendar for the voluntary fire-fighting service, cold-calling local businesses and asking them for money. This was perhaps the worst venture of all. One of the guys in the office would stroll in at half nine, make a few light-hearted banterous phone calls and then spend the rest of the day practising his putting on the carpet, being the living incarnation of all things chilled and content having apparently chocked up his sales quota for the day in those few easy morning minutes. I didn't buy it. With hindsight I'm not convinced that my first ever call had genuinely led to a sale either, but I kept plugging away on the basis of this small success and the example this other man set for all us aspiring leeches.

By the end of the week I was losing heart. The boss deployed his best psychology when he implied that I might not have 'the right stuff', but then he turned good cop and gave me his golden nugget piece of advice in a tone of voice that suggested I was being gifted with special powers:

'When you hear an actual 'No' on the line, when you hear that word… that's when you hit them with the killer line…'

I waited with great expectation for the transfer of secret powers to begin…

'You say this… don't you want to help us save lives?'

That was obviously the end of that.

Desperately needing something reliable and engaging

and at the very least, morally neutral, we settled on fruit picking, as much through a lack of options or imagination as anything else. But we had a plan! We had a focus. Before we could up-sticks and leave though, we had Christmas and New Year to attend to.

Christmas on the other side of the world is an unusual affair. Obviously there's no snow falling and it's the middle of summer, but you still see all the cards with snowmen on them and people still sing the season-specific carols: '*the weather outside is frightful, but the fire is so delightful, and since we've nowhere to go, let it snow.*' Absurd. And of course there's no family, which is what the festival time is all about. So you make do with what you've got. You make your own family. Or you borrow one. I was invited back to Cerys' house, which I gladly did, like a pinball or one of those balls on the end of a string that you bat ferociously until it eventually snaps off and you get on with something else. Her Mum bought me some nice red boxer shorts. We ate lots of chicken. I found myself alone in the house one afternoon with Cerys' ex-boyfriend for half an hour, which was awkward. I wasn't sure how to feel, for him or for myself. Some of Cerys' friends came round one day and we endured a few hours of having nothing in common and nothing to say to each other.

For New Year I headed back to the city and we threw a party with some of the guys Rob had befriended at work. It was a drunken, messy affair that started with vodka and concluded with me lying on the floor quietly fascinated by the way the carpet looked like a miniature mountain range beneath the open door. Perhaps I fell, or maybe I just needed an urgent nap. I don't remember. When somebody pushed on the door, this little mountain range was torn asunder and the illusion was over. The image lingered with me long enough to write a weird story about it that ended up being my first ever piece of published fiction in a collection of short stories. My mother bought plenty of copies and passed them on to her Irish family but my aunties banned them due to inappropriate content. My story, odd as it may have been, was not particularly disturbing to them, but some of the other stories in the collection were considered rude, lewd or offensive in some way. This small success and subsequent furore gave me an insight into the potential pitfalls of writing, aside from the obvious risk of being blacklisted by association in some countries. An old girlfriend's mother read it and asked if I'd ever expressed any suicidal tendencies. Somebody else brought the same question up right in front of me. I read back over it recently and cannot for the life of me think why. Weird, I learned, could sometimes be misinterpreted for miserable, but isn't it the job of a writer to go to weird places, to camp out a little beyond the norm, to explore the shadowy hinterlands of human experience and report back on them in an interesting and entertaining way, or even, if they're really good or really lucky, with something genuinely poetic and mind-expanding?

As soon as New Year was done with and the hangovers had all dissipated into the hot air, we packed up our kit and got the hell out of Melbourne to make some money. Where better to go than to the shadowy hinterlands?

5 THE CLOSEST THING TO PRISON

Off we went. Backwards.

Fruit picking is not only a guaranteed source of income derived from hearty labour set in the celebrated beauty of the Australian countryside (as we were led to believe)… it was also an adventure (as we were also led to believe)! Suddenly we were out of the city and back on the road, driving through the night in a packed bus as if we were bombing through the Sumatran jungle in search of Orang-utans or hurtling towards the thousand islands of Laos (without the pigs by our feet or the haze of chicken piss dribbling through the roof). We were living the dream again, filling our balloons and letting the winds take us. Woohoo!!! Life had a soundtrack that was optimistic again. Anything was possible. Anything could happen.

Within five minutes of our arrival at 'the compound', Rob and I were exchanging apprehensive looks and Jane was slumped on the bed in tears.

The accommodation was a cell in a terrace of breeze-block cells with hewn chunks of foam for mattresses on metal beds, a few steel lockers and little else except for a bare and oppressively over-bright light-bulb. Aside from the rudimentary nature of the quarters, it was the graffiti that had finally drawn the tears from Jane. Everywhere you looked, aggressive and racist epithets had been daubed on the walls. Above the door, a life size drawing of a woman had been scrawled with her legs spread wide, her genitals splayed out and a lascivious expression on her face that was willing you to either draw closer or run away, depending on your temperament and habits.

Fruit picking in the heart of Australia is a good way to find out how you might cope should you ever be sent to prison on false charges. It's also a great place to brush up on your casual racism, a skill that can easily be lost in the real world where most people try to treat other people as other people regardless of where they come from or what they look like. In such places, it is good to get your head down and do the work. Pick those peaches and pears, fill the punnets, take the money and run. On the first day, I managed one and a half bins. That's less than twenty-five dollars - nothing. We were size-picking pears, which meant you couldn't just grab every piece of fruit you could see. If too many small ones found their way into your bin, the 'ganger' would give you a dressing down. Over a certain threshold, he'd take the bin off your tally and you wouldn't get paid for them. It took a while to get used to what was acceptable and what was not, and even when that had become clear, the frustration of having to think before picking was infuriating when you're trying to go as fast as you can. Each picker had their own metal stepladder that needed to be carried around all day and plonked beneath the trees. A good picker would strip a tree with only a few placements of the ladder, but learning the trees was another art that took some time to master. Inexperienced pickers tended to waste time moving their ladder from placement to placement and going up and down it with half filled bags. The bag was strung across the shoulders so that it hung by your chest, like a backwards backpack. A frontpack. When it was full to the brim, descending the ladder was anything but straightforward.

Aside from the tricks that had to be mastered, you needed to be strong to cart the ladder around and go up and down it all day with sacks of pears. It was exhausting. Poor Jane struggled to fill half a bin on the first day. Rob was optimistic, taller and tougher than I, but he didn't fare much better. By the time we returned to our breeze block cell and hung up our picking bags, both taking the money and running with it seemed like impossible dreams.

Some of the other pickers that day filled seven punnets by noon and then buggered off to relax in the shade, smoking cigarettes and drinking tinnies. I assumed they were either mutant superheroes or technologically augmented humans, but I later discovered their grim secret: they boshed methamphetamine at 5am. This allowed them to pick with a rate of motion normally reserved for ravers until noon, after which it made perfect sense for them to sidle away to chill-out zones and drink themselves bonkers until sleep whisked them to somewhere better. This they did on a daily basis. They took weekends off. After six months on the picking trail they all had wads of cash and bodies that were outwardly chiselled and lean but inwardly soiled and tremulous. I have no idea what state their minds were in.

There were two subcategories of bonkers meth-picker, differentiated from one another by the way in which they spent the other half of the year, when the picking season was out. Some used their hard-won lucre to live the quiet highlife, surfing some far away distant paradise, zenning out with the ocean, maybe making music or writing but generally doing very little at all. Others transferred straight to the offshore fishing boats and followed the exact same routine for another six months with cod and haddock taking the place of pears and peaches. The latter were either supposedly saving for projects more ambitious than surfing, such as buying a place or retiring at forty. Some of them probably achieved this. Others had clearly become trapped in their desperate cycle of hedonism and hard labour. We gave them a wide birth; anyone who boshes amphetamine on a daily basis needs space and consideration, but on one occasion we got too close.

Rob had made friends with some pickers from another farm. I can't remember how or even who they were, but they invited us all to their static caravan park, off-site, a few miles down one endlessly straight road, followed by a few miles down another seemingly endless straight road at right angles to the first. How long-distance drivers don't fall asleep in Australia is a question I've never answered. The evening started off pleasantly, drinking tinnies outside, eating meat, chatting about this, that and whatever. As the sun went down, the weed came out and the mood shifted. I was sat at the table with a guy at least eighteen times bigger than me who had just arrived and was proceeding to build an over-sized joint out of three or four papers.

"Where are you from?" I asked, as you do. He came from Liverpool. That's Liverpool in Australia, not in the UK, but finding some common ground, I excitedly told him I was from near Liverpool too, and made some glib comment about car stereos. His reply was blunt. He told me that he couldn't stand people who made a big thing about where they come from, as if it determines who they are, or what they are, or what they might have in common with someone else. He wasn't Liverpudlian! He was him. Everything else was circumstantial. He was actually angry. And menacing in his anger. I felt like telling him he was a tosser, and I would have if I hadn't been slightly terrified and increasingly paranoid from the mad stuff they were rolling with. I'm generally a lightweight when it comes to smoking and I tend not to indulge much. These guys were stuffing handfuls of smash-your-mind skunkweed into bulging papers and serving it out freely. Rob was loving it. He could obviously handle it and seemed oblivious to the occasional darkening of the mood in the caravan. Jane was looking a bit pasty and restless. I felt like somebody was hitting me over the head with a cricket bat. Meanwhile the guy from the other Liverpool that has no connection to mine was throwing back beers at a similar rate to his rolling, which was impressively fast. He was also becoming increasingly short-tempered and spiky.

Eventually Jane and I managed to get the message through the fug to Rob that we both wanted to go, and so we initiated a shambolic departure. Of course we had no way of getting home ourselves, so Rob's friend said he'd drive us. Only he couldn't drive, a fact he amazingly managed to forget for a few stoned moments. Were there any taxis? The guy from Liverpool stood up. I like to keep calling him that. He grabbed his keys.

"I'll drive you back."

Rob smiled. His mate smiled and patted him on the back. They grabbed their coats and started to leave. I looked at Jane. She looked at me. We didn't say anything. We followed them out. They got in the car. We got in the back seat. The box of frogs from Liverpool was in front of me in the driver seat, Rob's friend in the passenger seat, then Rob behind him and Jane in the middle. Off we went. Backwards. It sounds contrived, but this genuinely happened. The idiot put the car in reverse instead of drive and backed into the caravan. This was hilarious, apparently, judging by the reaction of everyone in the car aside from Jane and I. We shared another glance that said as clear as day what we both knew - we should be getting out of the car. Off we went. Forwards this time, lurching around the winding lanes of the caravan park and out onto the highway. I've never been so grateful for the straightness of a road. The Liverpudlian had a tinnie open and was still drinking it, jabbering away as he did, but he kept the car straight until we reached the junction, whereupon he swung it through ninety degrees and headed straight again. So far so good. We'd be home in no time, safe and sound. Then he slammed the brake on and we skidded in the road as we came to a sudden stop, the car lying diagonal, half on one side of the central line, half on the other, headlights illuminating a tunnel of emptiness by the side of the road. The engine purred and metal ticked and creaked. What the hell had happened? The thought had occurred to our friendly Liverpudlian that it might be nice to have another joint for the ride. Another moment of hilarity ensued as he cobbled together a skunk stogie and downed the rest of his beer amid great banter and whooping. Rob was still loving it, but I could tell that Jane was feeling about as happy as I was about being in the car with these guys, with a driver very much under the influence of something narcotic, perhaps psychotic.

By the time he finally resumed his driving duties, a pair of lights had appeared in the distance ahead, another car approaching us. He turned the wheel and took us back in the right direction, then he floored it and we started going faster and faster. I couldn't see the speedometer but I knew it was only limited by the acceleration of the car, that he was giving it all he could with the pedal all the way down. The sickly stench of skunk was filling the car. Jane dug her fingers into my thigh. I dug my own fingers into the fascia of the door, gripping the handle as if I could squeeze into something else, something more useful and less inert, like a teleportation device perhaps. The Liverpudlian drifted us into the middle of the road and continued his march towards the car's top speed. He was roaring now. The guy in the passenger seat was whooping. Rob was shouting, but it was hard to tell why and whether it was supportive or in protest. The other car drew closer. Was this going to be it? Death at the hands of a drunk and stoned driver on the straightest road in the world? Was he suicidal? Was he playing chicken or did he have something more macabre planned for us all? At the speed we were now going it would take nothing more than a freaky synapse or a moment of presumed hilarity for him to jerk the wheel and send us into a roll. Anything could happen in the hands of this madman. And I'd got in the car.

Nobody had forced me. We were screaming towards the headlights. The idiots were screaming too. Inside I was screaming. Jane was stock still in her seat, staring between the front seats at her future, gripping my leg as if by doing so she could hold onto her past. At the last minute, we swerved back to the right side of the road and flew passed the other car, which didn't alter its direction in the slightest. The driver either had nerves of steel or was as obliviously inebriated as our driver was. Maybe everybody was like this. Maybe it was normal. The horn gradually quietened in the wake of our engine. The Liverpudlian eased off the accelerator and we dropped down to a normal speed. We turned in to the farm. We got out of the car. We said goodbye. We went to bed. We woke up. Still alive.

It took us a while but we got to grips with the work eventually, or at least we found our different ways. Jane wrangled a transfer to the conveyor belts where she spent the day picking out bum pears from an endless carousel of knobbly fruit. It was mind-numbing stuff with the din and moan of industrial machinery, but better for her than going up and down the ladders. Rob and I developed some shoulders and raised our daily punnet count to make enough on a daily basis to make it sort of worthwhile. I had a lucky break too, getting a serious dose of sunburn in the second week that would normally lead to a picker being unceremoniously dumped from the roster. There's no room for weakness in the outback; if you can't pick, you're out. But instead of booting me out they transferred me for a few days to a metal roller, like a lawnmower with a metre-long magnet instead of blades. My job was to trundle up and down the roads and tracks picking up nails and anything else metallic that might find its way into a tyre and pop it. I was cleaning roads! In the closest place I'd ever known to prison. I was tempted to draw arrows on my shirt, clamp my legs in irons and start singing work songs. But I was still there, and for that I should have been gracious. I wasn't.

During the first morning I stumbled upon a concealed area of woodland that was home to three wrecked cars. The ground was strewn with metallic bits and bobs that filled the roller up in a few paces. Pleased with the hard labour of those few paces, I sat down for a while in the shade of a tree and chewed on some yellow grass. After all that strenuous effort, I naturally deserved a break. The sky was wide and blue. Insects buzzed around and birds occasionally flapped and tweeted above me. The distant sound of labour carried on a gentle breeze, but otherwise it was quiet in the copse. In the lazy heat a cunning plan formed ever so slowly and with the greatest of ease in my mind. I tarried there for another ten minutes before returning to the main shed and dumping my load of dangerous nails. I waved at the other workers. I tipped my hat to the boss in his pokey office at the back. Then I waltzed back out with my machine and headed straight for the automotive graveyard and the tree that had so kindly supported my back and provided me with shade from the mid-morning sun. At lunchtime I popped back to my room to get The Analects of Confucius, and that's how I spent the next three days, sitting in the shade of a tree reading Chinese philosophy.

Meanwhile Jane was enjoying her own dose of good fortune and thanks to her we managed to escape our breezeblock apartment and move in with a couple that lived in the nearby town. The woman worked alongside Jane on the belts. I'll call her Francis. Francis was a big woman and she could be intimidating when she felt the urge. She was in charge, and her partner - I'll call him George – really had very little chance of ever matching her in any sort of power struggle, be it physical or otherwise. He was English but had moved to Australia believing the climate would more conducive to good health. He only had half his guts, or maybe less, and that isn't meant in any metaphorical or figurative sense. He was a timid but likeable fellow who played computer games and pretty much did what he was told. They were nice people, odd in a small-town-nothing-ever-happens-except-possibly-the-most-depraved-thing-you-can-ever-imagine way. We wondered what they got up to when we weren't around, but our wondering made us all a little uneasy, so we stopped. They were certainly generous, taking only token contributions from us as rent, which allowed us to actually save some money.

Rob and Jane left after a month, their purses refilled and their patience straining. They headed back to Asia, this time to China. I stayed on for a while. Rob confessed he was concerned for me. Being left alone in that strange place, who knows what might happen? Francis might taker me as another husband and lock me in a cupboard or tie me to a bed in an out-building somewhere for her terrible amusement. I wasn't exactly sure what I was doing anymore or why, and it was weird when Rob and Jane left, so I left too. I'd grown used to having them around, which is odd for a couple. Normally you feel like a third wheel, but I hadn't really felt like that at all. And besides, I had a bit of money. Not enough to do anything really amazing or last for very long out there in the world, but I had some, and it gave me freedom to indulge in my rudderlessness.

I headed back to Melbourne and used up another two weeks of conservation volunteerism that I'd paid for back in England. It's worth picking that sentence apart to pin down the absurdity… 'volunteerism'… 'paid for'. I had a birthday while I was paying to volunteer. I spent the day burning aloe vera with strangers. Then I went to see Cerys again. She was happy to see me. I was happy to see her. Deep down we both knew that it was over, but we weren't old enough to know that most damage happens in the part of a relationship that comes after this realisation and before 'the end'. So we hooked up again, hired a car and drove the Great Ocean Road from Melbourne round to Queensland. We made it half way before we had to turn around. I started blowing money, as if I had a pathological reason to do so. Perhaps the romanticism of the broke traveller had got to me. I went horse riding on the beach. The spiritless animal ignored me the whole time, refusing to treat me as anything more than a bag of bones that needed carting from one place to another. All my cowboy dreams were insulted and rubbished by this miserable animal, but I had sympathy for his position. He was as much a bag of bones as I was, but for him it was an every-day gig. I went aerobatic flying in an old bi-plane, loop the looping and stall-diving. I expected it to be like a fairground ride with sudden jolts and rushes and g-forces. It turned out to be a very gentle affair, slow and serene and not at all whizzy or fast. My internal organs eased themselves up into my ribcage and squished into each other, then eased their way back down and slumped into my belly. Very strange feeling. I remembered why I never enjoyed flight simulators as a kid – they were always so monotonously slow. I guess that's what it's like.

At the end of the road we camped up by the Southern Ocean and made love for the last time, both of us trying to make it all right for the other, but both of us knowing that it wasn't and wouldn't be. Afterwards I walked down to the shoreline in the dark. The moon was almost full and I could see the flicking manes of the white horses, but at ten feet away, I stopped and couldn't go any further. The deep bass boom of the only ocean that goes all the way round the world without once breaking on land had me gripped by its power. It sounded like continental plates grinding against one another, like the pounding of mythic gods on the gates to the underworld. It sounded and felt massive, and by contrast I felt small in a good way, in a way that meant everything was going to be okay. At that moment I heard a voice clear as light in my head: go home.

Next morning we turned back and headed towards Melbourne. I dropped Cerys at her parent's house and we said goodbye. She slipped an envelope into my hand as I left and I opened it in a car park a few miles down the road. There was a note about angels. I read it. There was a picture too. She was striking an alluring pose. Strangely, perhaps due to the unusual angle or the lighting or a trick of time, I didn't recognise her.

I dropped the car off and stood on a street corner in Melbourne, waiting for whimsy or a gust of wind to take me somewhere. People were milling around, talking, looking around, drinking coffee, rushing to and fro or idling along pavements. A group accumulated on the edge of the road and stood there waiting for a senseless green man to tell them to cross. There was no traffic. I resisted the urge to shout at them, to implore them to think for themselves. And there I was, waiting for the wind.

I was now properly broke again and I wanted to go home. I couldn't because my ticket had expired and I'd spent the money I needed to replace it on my guitar. Then I'd spent the money I'd earned in the closest thing to prison on foolhardy adventures. I could probably have borrowed some cash from somebody, a friend, my sister, but I'd already taken the cash for the car from my father and I didn't want to go begging for any more from anyone. I called the picking farm. The pears had gone. They were on peaches. Without much enthusiasm I headed back to Francis and George's to do one more month of picking.

This time round it was just about getting my head down and making the money. Peach picking is horrible if you happen to be sensitive to the chemicals that get stuck in the fluff. Your face swells up and goes red and you itch and itch. I didn't care. I just wanted to get out of there and picking those furry peaches was the way to do it. In three weeks I was knackered and my face was a red balloon but I had enough dollars to buy the ticket. I logged on to the internet to book the ticket, but while I was waiting for the booking system to load I checked my emails and found a surprise waiting there in my inbox, the kind of surprise that pumps air back into adventure balloons and sets the dice rolling for rudderless trajectories – just my kind of surprise. The Pisces Hill Writing Retreat had offered me a place to stay and work on my novel. Free accommodation. Free board. For how long? Initially three weeks. Could it be? One last adventure before home…

6 PISCES HILL

Erm, I don't really want to.

Pisces Hill was an old farm in the hills north of Canberra. It was run by a man I shall call Keith. He was originally an English diplomat, presumably very respectable, aristocratic and silver-spooned, a buffoon perhaps, or a noble officer-soldier type. As a young man in China he had a spectacular idea that changed his life in an unimaginable way. He wrote some English textbooks. They were used throughout China, and they were pretty much the first ones in circulation. China is a big place. The cheques it writes are accordingly big too. In no time at all he became a self-made man, a man of leisure, the sort that can live by whimsy and has the wherewithal to act upon it. Pisces Hill was one such whim. To build it he enlisted the help of Paula and Pete, an industrious and enthusiastic couple who had previously toured Australia in an old school van they'd converted themselves. It had a sauna-bath and a cute red kit car that rolled out of the back like Knight Rider. Pete raced it sometimes on tracks. They both played in folk bands. They had kids, grown up and gone. Aside from being the Australian model-airplane aerobatics champion,

Pete was also an architect and builder who specialised in zero-impact homes integrated into the natural environmental, the kind of homes that can survive bush fires and don't need to be plugged in. The guy was incredible, so much so that I doubted he was human in any real sense of the word, but incredibly talented and industrious without the slightest trace of hubris or conceit. He designed and built the retreat and managed the grounds while Paula managed all the other aspects of its daily running, including writing the advert that I'd sent a speculative reply to months before.

I paid Keith an initial fee of fifteen dollars. I can't remember exactly what this was for, some kind of token transaction for the accounts perhaps. I stayed there for three weeks. There were no other writers so I had the retreat all to myself. Every morning fresh oranges were delivered for squeezing and fresh coffee was brewed up. Lunches and dinners were provided and the freezer and fridge were always full and available to me. They always had good quality chorizo. I had a computer in my room and the retreat space had a communal living area with a television, a video library and various musical instruments. I'd work in the mornings then go quad-biking with Pete or fly his planes, sit on the veranda and chat with Paula or take a wander through the grounds and watch kangaroos bounding through the woods.

At lunchtimes Keith would appear from his private residence and provide us with a meal. He was an exceptional cook and each and every dish was delightful, but on the days that he was unable to do this, Paula would step in and deputise. She confided in me one day that whenever she was asked to this, she had to make a point of deliberately underperforming in the kitchen. Keith was sensitive – he prided himself on his culinary expertise and didn't like to be shown up. I felt this was all fairly ridiculous, behaving in such a way when you're a self-made man of leisure, but when a woman called Wednesday

Kennedy arrived, a similar reaction resulted in me being unceremoniously booted out a week early! More of that later. I shouldn't complain. When I arrived I was twenty thousand words into my first novel and trying to work out how the hell it was going to all fit together, where it was going and what in fact it was. When I left three weeks later the research from Melbourne had alchemised into another twenty thousand words and my ideas were far more focused and clear. I knew what I was doing. Sort of. At least, I knew what to do next, which is sometimes half the battle.

In the evenings I'd often work late and sometimes while away the early hours watching a video or just tootling on my guitar. One night I made the terrible mistake of watching Deliverance on my own, for the first time, with no expectation of *that scene.* My sleep was fitful afterwards, but morning came and the whole splendid routine repeated.

Days passed by easily in this manner. I became very friendly with Paula and Pete, but Keith remained elusive. He stayed in his quarters most of the time and I'd only see him at lunch times. When we did speak we got along well. He was interested in the book I was writing and he enjoyed talking to me about literature and the art and craft of scribbling, something I was particularly geeky about at the time. I enjoyed hearing about the unusual life he had led. One day we drove into town together to do some shopping, which is not something he normally did. He bought the post office. He'd already bought the barbershop and was renting it back to the owners for a nominal cent or two, apparently as a gesture of goodwill to the local community. This was not unusual for a man who combined generosity with a sort of child-like enthusiasm for whatever fell under the spotlight of his whimsy. On one very surreal day a van full of Alpacas arrived at the farm. They had come all the way from Peru and seemed as bemused as the gardener who did his best to cater for them. They were eventually shipped back, hapless victims of a distant gentleman's faddish notions. He was a true man of leisure Keith, a dabbler, a patron, a builder of romantic and pointless follies.

Easter arrived and Paula and Pete announced they would be leaving the retreat to visit family. I was told that I should leave too, as there'd be nobody to look after me. Suggesting that I might be able to look after myself seemed like a reasonable thing to do, but it also seemed fairly obvious, after all, I had managed to look after myself in Asia for nine months without freshly squeezed orange juice or central heating. I was welcome to come back and finish out the month after the break, I was told, but where would I go in the meantime? Paula and Pete understood my predicament and interceded with Keith to convince him to let me stay, on the understanding that I would be to some extent capable of supporting myself. I'd still get lunch made for me. Keith was softening in his stance towards me, even inviting me to drink wine with him and a lady friend of his, an author from Sydney. Then Wednesday Kennedy arrived and it all went downhill. Fast.

Wednesday was a poet, performer, artist and filmmaker in her early forties. She arrived at Pisces Hill from New York where she'd been performing a one-woman show. When the twin towers came down she went bombing around the streets interviewing anyone who would talk to her about it, recording everything with a camcorder and a Dictaphone. She returned to Pisces Hill to compile the material with a view to making a film and radio piece. She also come to see Keith, her benefactor who'd provided the funds for the original trip to New York and would now be providing her the space and freedom to work with the material she'd accumulated. The exact nature of their relationship revealed itself when I was invited into Keith's private quarters for dinner on the night of Wednesday's arrival. This was unheard of – nobody went in to the private quarters of Keith. Perhaps Wednesday had persuaded him. Perhaps he felt sorry for me. Perhaps he'd decided he liked me. I wish I hadn't gone in!

Aside from the bedroom and the bathroom, everything was open plan. A pristine white baby grand piano stood on a raised stage in one corner. The walls were floor to ceiling shelves with books packed in tight, old ones, new ones, fiction, poetry, philosophy, reference… all kinds of books. The furniture was all immaculate. Artefacts from far-flung places were scattered deliberately around.

The three of us sat at one end of a large table of dark hardwood. A three-pronged candelabra was lit as a centrepiece. Antique place mats were marshalled by neatly placed and well-polished cutlery. Crystal cut wine glasses were filled with expensive wine and the chatter was all about New York. Dinner was fish pie, one of Keith's specialties. The pomp with which it was laid down and presented to us implied that much time and effort had gone into its preparation. I was complimentary in my appraisal of its merit. A fine fish pie. Really quite excellent.

As the evening went on, the psycho-geography of the relationship between Keith and Wednesday became clearer to me. He provided her with funds. She provided him with an eternally unrequited promise of the elusive feminine principle. He was a 70-year-old man. She was a 43-year-old woman, a strong one, sexy, independent, complicated and unattainable. I was a naïve 23-year-old man, green around the gills and a complete ingénue when it came to the kind of games they were playing. Without realising, I became part of the game, simply because of my age and gender. After a bottle or two of wine, Keith started to tire. Wednesday started to light up. She took another bottle from the kitchen and told me to follow her. We were going to stay up and watch the video footage. She had some weed, she said. We could pull an all-nighter. I could feel Keith bristling, but he was worn out and he knew he would not keep up. 'Erm, I don't really want to', would have been a good reply, but I just waddled out behind her and we drank the wine, smoked her weed and watched the footage until dawn. It was all pretty messy, but fascinating. At first. After a few hours, it all sounded the same. I admired Wednesday. She scared the hell out of me but she was exciting to be around, a strong-willed woman who seemed all broken up inside but was not taking any crap from anyone. She smoked cigarettes like she was eating them.

Paula and Pete returned the next day. As the sun was dying the woods pink, Paula asked me if I was ready to go, all packed up? Did I need any help getting to the station? I didn't understand.

"I don't understand," I said.

"Keith said you'd decided to leave, that you were going tomorrow," she replied.

We looked at each other with incomprehension for some time until I explained that I had made no such decision. Perhaps Keith had, I suggested. She asked me if I wanted to leave. No I didn't. My flight wasn't for another few days and I was still as broke as I'd been before I arrived. I had nowhere to go, and to be honest, I was through with travel. I just wanted to jump on the plane and be gone. I explained what had happened with Wednesday, how I'd become something like a pawn in a game I only half understood. Paula confirmed my suspicions, reminding me about her deliberate bad cooking at lunch times and implying as politely as possible what I already knew. The relationship between Wednesday and Keith was complicated and she'd used me to fire up the complications, simply because I was a young man and he wasn't. He hadn't liked it one bit. The solution – get rid of me. So I was unceremoniously booted out.

I met Keith shortly before my departure and he shook my hand and mumbled something about good luck and all the best, but it was clear from his demeanour that he was uncomfortable. He knew he was shafting me for undignified reasons, but I'd only paid fifteen dollars in the first place and I'd lived there for 3 weeks, drinking all the fresh orange juice and coffee I could drink, eating lush fish pies, hanging out with Paula and Pete, getting good work done, chasing kangaroos and whizzing about on quads, flying model airplanes with a champion… I was incredibly grateful to him and I told him so. I was angry with Wednesday, but I didn't see her again. I kept my eyes out for a movie, but never found one.

7 FROM HERO TO VILLAIN

That's what it's all about Dave.

I hit the road and headed towards the airport, albeit in no great haste because I had time to fill. I have no recollection of the name of the town I ended up in. It had a fantastic bakery from which I bought some rolls to supplement the stick of chorizo and the bag of rice I already had, last minute gifts from Paula. I trundled up to a hostel with my bag and my beautiful guitar and asked in my most humble voice if I might be able to stay there for not much money at all. The manager was neither amenable to be taken advantage of nor generous in spirit. The compromise we struck was that I could use the kitchen to make my rice and then I could sleep outside. I had foolishly told her in the negotiation that I had a tent. It was a mosquito net tent, which means mosquito netting held up by a pole with a ground sheet sewn around the bottom. A Danish guy who'd infuriated me with a nauseating catch phrase in Thailand had given me it… 'That's what's all about Dave.' For example…

"Hey Dave, what have you been up to?"

"Oh I just I rented a bike and drove down the Burmese

border for a few weeks."

"That's what it's all about Dave."

It wasn't so bad hearing this all the time, but when he borrowed Wanderings by Herman Hesse, a book I had planned to keep for the duration of the trip and dip in and out of as I went along, he disappeared for two weeks with it. When he reappeared he blithely told me he'd passed it on to somebody else. I was about to go nuts, which is something I don't often do. He got in first with his catchphrase: that's what it's all about Dave! No it bloody well isn't. I swore at him with more colourful language than I'm comfortable repeating here. Our reunion was a chance encounter anyway – he should never have gone away with it in the first place. That's when he gave me the tent, though it was broken when he gave it to me and I had to gaffer-tape the pole and have it stitched. To make matters worse my sleeping bag was designed for the tropics and winter was coming around again in Australia. If he'd been there with me at that moment he probably would have said it again… That's what it's all about Dave. NO IT ISN'T. I would probably have punched him.

I made my rice, par-boiled and then fried up with the chorizo. As the sun edged out of the sky and into the desert interior, I headed out into the night and tried to get to sleep before the real cold came out. No chance. It was already freezing. I'm not averse to the cold, and I can handle it to a degree, but that night was insufferable. I'd lie there trying to sleep but my bones would start to freeze with the ground, so I'd have to turn and put other bones in contact with the ground, but within minutes, they'd freeze so I'd have to move again. I lay there executing a wriggling dance of discomfort in my hopelessly ill-suited bag and tent, wishing that I knew of a way to lie without allowing any part of one's body to touch the ground. I needed to levitate, but such skills were beyond me.

I tried to distract myself with storytelling, recounting tales of derring-do and close shaves along the road, like the bus station in Udon Thani where I found myself stranded at 2:30am and had to wait for two hours for the next bus. I had to get cash out from the machine and as I was walking back to the station with more money than some of the locals would make in months, three men circled behind me and then called to me:

"Ay Farang, You Muay Thai?"

Farang meant foreigner. Muay Thai meant kickboxing. I don't kickbox, at least not very well. I didn't really want to start either, so I deployed my best Thai colloquialisms, smiled as smilingly as I could (which was what they advise in the guidebooks), laughed, turned and continued on my way. I think the bad Thai confounded them. I told them I was 'not pineapple'. An old tea-dude in Pai assured me this was a colloquial expression for being rubbish at something. He might have been winding me up, but it got me back to the safety of the station lights. I bought some Pringles and chocolate for the ticket counter staff and they let me sleep inside, safe beneath one of the desks. The memory didn't warm me up much.

Three weeks into my travels, I awoke to find an itchy bite on my thigh. By the end of the day I had loads of them, all over my leg, spreading from the first, raised and puffy red blotches. I moved out of my room and took the tent down to the river, thinking that being in a more natural environment with clean river air would be better for me. In the early hours of the morning, just beyond the witching hour, I awoke again to find my entire body full of the red blotches. Head to foot. And inside too – my mouth was itchy and my throat was closing up. My breath was laboured. Anaphylactic shock. But I didn't even know about anaphylaxis back then, having never encountered it before. For all I knew this was some obscure and incurable tropical disease that was going to do me in three weeks into my grand adventure. Some of my friends had told me I was mad for going off on my own. One such pal drily told me that we no longer need to travel – we have natural history shows on television. A week before I left, my Dad pointed out that I may as well have had a bull's-eye painted on my forehead; carrying all my fancy western clobber made me an obvious target. One of many.

I lurched out of the tent and took stock of my situation. River. Footpath. Nearby huts. I should have gone and banged on a nearby hut. I knew some guys who were in the ones close by, but instead I started walking. There was a hospital here somewhere, on the outskirts. I'd seen it on a map, along one of the main roads. I was in Pai – there were only two or three main roads to choose from. I headed up the path. My throat closed a little more with every step. There was nobody out on the streets, and a bizarre alter-culture of canines was being played out. The tough dogs owned the central crossroads and main streets, and they patrolled them and policed them. The further you went from the centre, the more mangy and weak they became, until at the very edge of town you have multiple dogs on the same corners, padding around fearfully, though there were no other dogs beneath them in the hierarchy.

I was delirious when I reached the hospital.

'I… can't… breathe…'

They weighed me. Took my height. Asked me questions for what seemed like forever.

'I… can't… breathe…'

One of the nurses laughed. She actually laughed. Not maliciously. It was the laugh of a humouring mother when their child is being dramatic for no reason. But I couldn't breathe! They prepped a needle. What was it? Adrenalin. I had no idea why adrenalin would help me or what it would do, but what choice did I have? Turns out it was exactly what was required. Once injected the nurse told me I could leave. I told her I couldn't. She laughed again. Could I sleep there? She laughed again and found me a blanket. I crashed on a wooden bench and woke up completely free of any blotches, my throat clear, my breathing easy. The nurse squeezed in another giggle as she confirmed that I was fine and there was nothing to worry about. I retraced my steps past all the dogs, but they'd gone, replaced by people who kicked at them and threw things if they came too close. I was alive! The sun was sparkling in a blue sky! People were smiling at me! But that was long ago. I was still freezing in my stupid mosquito net tent and no amount of rolling was making it better.

At about 2am, I gave up and snuck inside. The crime-fighter superhero became the criminal… this time it was I who was breaking into the hostel.

The common room was quiet but for a humming fridge. I craved softness, and the sofas looked so enticing. Had I not already asked and been told in no uncertain terms that I could not stay in the hostel without paying, I couldn't just plonk myself on the cushions. I climbed over one, squeezed down beside the wall and lay down wedged between the back of a sofa and the wall. The carpet was made of clouds; warm fluffy ones that are soft to the touch. I fell asleep easily, into a lovely sleep, the sort you saviour drifting into and have no desire to leave. It must have been dusty there, because when I finally did wake up the first thing I wanted to do was sneeze. I was about to, when I heard voices nearby and smelt the bacon. The common room was full of people eating their breakfast. I heard the voice of the warden too. I couldn't sneeze. I was desperate to, but I couldn't, so I lay there holding it in until the coast was clear.

In the bakery that morning I met a couple of French girls who had a room in the hostel. Their room had four beds, two of which were empty. They thought it was hilarious that I had managed to stay hidden behind the sofa for well over an hour, not sneezing once, and had then successfully snuck back out without being caught. In return for a few songs, they snuck me into their room that night and I slept so deep I may have died for a short time.

The next day, I headed to the airport and flew out of

there. I left my jumper in the bakery, the same bobbly jumper I'd carried around the world with me for eighteen months, the only one I'd carried around, and the only item of clothing I'd managed to keep hold of. You get attached to such things when you have so few possessions for so long. Sleeping bags that you've slept in hundreds of times become familiar places, the closest thing to a home you have when you live out of a bag. The backpack becomes an extension of your body by being strapped to your back for so long. T-shirts become second skins. Trainers mould so well to the contours of your feet that you no longer wear them. You inhabit them. My initial reaction to the loss of my jumper was intense sadness, almost desperate, as if this jumper had a soul that had been extinguished by its loss. It was time to get on the airplane and fly home. It was time to move on to the next chapter of my life. Time to lose the jumper.

"That's what it's all about Dave."

WHERE TO NEXT?

MEANDERINGS #2 "UNCHARTED TERRITORY"

Armed with useless information, a bag smaller than the one he took to school and minimal experience with a motorbike, David flies into Mandalay with a dream to ride the jungle trails of northern Burma. He ends up in a chicken farm. He briefly joins the gold rush. He slips unarmed into rebel-held territory. He falls for a girl called Snow who may or may not be what she appears to not be. Lost in the jungle in the dead of night with dying torch batteries he wonders if he's taken the idea of adventuring a little too far. Meanwhile, the shadowy echoes of a brutal regime are never too distant.

IF YOU LIKED THIS, PLEASE GO TO AMAZON AND LEAVE SOME KIND WORDS SO OTHER PEOPLE WILL KNOW!!!

WRITE FOR SIMPLEPIGEON???

When was the last time you climbed out of the window and disappeared?

We've all got tales to tell. Does one of yours shine an oblique light on the world of travel? Can you tell it in less than 20 000 words? If it fits the vision of simplepigeon, we might publish it. Initial contact by email to daid@talk21.com .

COMING SOON

SOULSTREAMERS

When a young boy from the valley of Streams accidentally devours the wrong fish and starts to hear whispers in the wind, he finds himself cast out of the village on a perilous and hilarious quest to find the other half of his soul. Pursued by sinister miracle hunters and ruthless businessmen, starved half to death in icy mountains and struck down by perplexing ailments, he could just go home, but the whispers will never leave him until he finds her… whoever she is.

SoulStreamers is a quixotic and light-hearted capering romp set in a world not too dissimilar to our own, one in which light can pour like water from the tips of mountains and the voices in your head, if you choose to trust them, can lead you to a love pre-destined and inevitable.

SoulStreamers is complete and ready for publishing.

ARE YOU A PUBLISHER? OR AN AGENT?

GET IN TOUCH IF YOU'D LIKE TO KNOW MORE.

COMING SOON

JACKS

"The work of the eyes is done. Go now and do the heart-work on the images imprisoned within you."

Maria Ranier Rilke

When Jack suddenly loses his sight at the wheel of his car, he'd rather think nothing of it and get on with his ordinary life, but a strange malady afflicts him. Episodes of sensory deprivation escalate until he finds himself in a hospital bed, his wife gone and his son tracing letters on the palm of his hand. When this final connection is severed, he drifts into steadily deteriorating landscapes of self and the struggle to return begins.

A literary mind-bender, a narrative fugue peppered with light touches, Jacks tells the astonishing story of an ordinary man's unintentional quest to understand love and find meaning in life in the face of the inevitable non-existence at the end of the universe.

Jacks is complete and ready for publishing.

ARE YOU A PUBLISHER? OR AN AGENT?

GET IN TOUCH IF YOU'D LIKE TO KNOW MORE.

COMING (AGAIN) SOON

THE MUSICIAN

Described by Chris Somerville (BBC) as a 'musical Da Vinci Code' and 'heartfelt, intense, a profound meditation on music', The Musician is a mesmerising story of a character trapped in another man's history and freed by revelations about the structure, the beauty and the very essence of music.

When Alex sets off for Asia he finds himself held by the melodies of a mysterious and primeval music. Guided by elusive backstreet characters and a trail of confusing symbols, he must unstitch the threads of an ancient Brotherhood to solve the riddle contained within him. He must become more than a Master of his own destiny.

The Musician was originally published in 2007 by Bluechrome as 'Music of Maninjau'. Shortly thereafter, Bluechrome disappeared - poooooof! – gone, leaving a raft of authors bobbing on stormy waters.

ARE YOU A PUBLISHER? OR AN AGENT?

GET IN TOUCH IF YOU'D LIKE TO KNOW MORE.

ABOUT THE AUTHOR

David Green was born in Southport in 1977. With no clear strategy for life, he spent four years studying Chemistry and Molecular Physics at Nottingham University, which paved the way for him to become a Physics teacher. In the meantime a chance encounter with one particular book made him pick up a guitar and start writing songs. Not long after that, the same book drove a pen into his hand, and he started writing books, often inspired by long trips out alone in the world, sometimes by long trips inwards.

Other projects can be explored on the website:

www.davegreen.org

ACKNOWLEDGMENTS

I'd like to thank all the characters that illuminated this chapter of life with fun, love and spirit. The names have been changed to protect the innocent, but you know who you are – Rob, Jane, Pete, Paula, Jim and his family, Keith, Francis and George, and particularly Cerys for whom there will always be a special place reserved in my affections.

Thanks too in particular to *apb* for support and encouragement and for talking me into doing something with 'the travel stuff'.

Thanks to everyone who has ever proof-read any of my stuff, particularly my father who is always on hand with red pen. I'll need you again.